Dynamic Assessing

The Assessor Survival Guide

Assessing in the Real World

Foreword

Although the author is from a construction background and has used his personal experiences as examples, the principles and practices outlined in this book are transferable throughout all disciplines where the assessment of Learners in the workplace is practiced.

Table of Contents

Introduction

Due to the challenging economic realities of recent years it has become essential that we all adapt to survive the changing financial climate.

The aim of this book is to enable assessors reduce the number of assessment visits they need to carry out whilst maintaining high standards of assessment.

To do this we must go back to basics and reassess the way in which we work.

We will look at the fundamental question of why we carry out assessments and investigate new ways of gathering our evidence including; *'Dynamic Assessing'*, *'Remote Assessing'*, and how we can embrace new technologies such as the internet, mobile phones and social media.

Following the simple theories outlined within this book the assessor will become more efficient and, not only maintain high success rates, but increase them.

Standard 9 Assess Learner Achievement

Before we go any further we must consider the National Occupational Standard for Assessing Learner Achievement.

This is the Standard that we all have to work to when assessing and it is the Standard that our internal and external quality advisors will judge us against.

The following is taken directly from National Occupational Standards for Learning and Development (Final version approved March 2010), Standard 9 Assess learner achievement.
This standard is about assessing learning and development against agreed criteria. It covers a range of different assessments including competence, knowledge and understanding and skills.

9.1 Ensure learners understand the purpose, requirements and processes of assessment

9.2 Plan assessment to meet requirements and learner needs

9.3 Use valid, fair, reliable and safe assessment methods

9.4 Identify and collect evidence that is: valid, authentic, sufficient

9.5 Make assessment decisions against specified

criteria

9.6 Provide feedback to the learner that affirms achievement and identifies any additional requirements

9.7 Maintain required records of the assessment process, its outcomes and learner progress

9.8 Work with others to ensure the standardisation of assessment practice and outcomes

Authentic	*The candidate's own work*
Reliable	*Consistently achieves the same results with the same (or similar) group of learners*
Requirements	*These could be the requirements of the practitioner's own organisation or those of an external organisation, such as awarding organisation*
Sufficient	*Enough evidence as specified in Evidence Requirements or Assessment Strategy.*
Valid	*Relevant to the criteria against which the candidate is being assessed.*
Fair	*Ensuring that everyone has an equal chance of getting an accurate assessment.*
Safe	*This covers both physical and psychological safety. It also includes ensuring that assessment evidence is safe in the sense that is sufficiently robust to make a reliable judgement that the learner does meet the assessment standard.*

Key Points

Look at each of the criteria of Standard 9 of the National Occupational Standards for Assessing Learner Achievement and see how you comply with them.

Consider if there are any ways you can improve your delivery to ensure you comply, for instance; having an induction checklist.

The Assessment Team

Assessment is best carried out by a team of people, working together, with the common aim of gathering sufficient evidence that is valid and safe to prove the Learner's competence.

The Assessment Team includes the assessor, the Learner, and the Learners' colleagues, supervisors, employers, and clients. It is vital to encourage all members of the team to help gather sufficient evidence to deem your Learner competent. Of course all evidence must meet the criteria of being authentic and relevant.

The Learner

The Learner is the most important member of the assessment team.

Given the necessary information, the Learner should be able identify suitable assessment opportunities for you to gather sufficient evidence to deem the Learner competent. Suitable assessment opportunities could include Product Evidence where the Learner is able to give you the contact details of witnesses who can authenticate the evidence. The Learner can also introduce you to a range of people who will be able to provide witness able to testify to their competence.

The Learner can also ask Colleagues to take photos or shoot videos of the Learner at work or ask clients, employers and supervisors for references which may be used as evidence. The Learner may be able to obtain copies of documents they have completed.

Another crucial role of the Learner, is to identifying times when rarely carried out operations are due to be performed, thereby enabling you to observe these rarely carried out tasks.

Colleagues

Colleagues are an often overlooked source of valuable evidence, because they are working with the Learner, colleagues are able to observe the Learner during the whole of the working day, from the moment they arrive at work until they leave. They can therefore provide witness testimonies for a wide range of criteria; from signing in in the morning, maintaining welfare facilities, appropriate communication with colleagues, and maintaining and storing tools and appropriate care and storage of personal protection equipment.

Colleagues can also authenticate Product Evidence and Professional Discussions.

In addition to helping you gather evidence, the Learner's colleagues form a valuable pool of potential Learners which can provide business for you and your Centre.

The Supervisor

The Supervisor is a very useful member of the team and it is essential that you keep the supervisor 'on board'.

We rely on the supervisor's goodwill to help us assess our Learners. The supervisor can arrange the work so that our Learner is carrying out the appropriate work at the time of our observation, so we don't make unnecessary journeys and wasting our time The supervisor can also grant the Learner time to discuss their progress on their qualification, plan future assessments and complete documentations.

The supervisor is in a position to identify work carried in the past and provide a Witness Testimony. The supervisor can also authenticate a Learner's Professional Discussion.

The supervisor is also a potential Learner and can identify other potential Learners.

The Employer

Generally, an employer wants all his staff to be qualified to the appropriate level. This can be a tremendous help when a Learner begins to lose enthusiasm, a word from their employer generally gives a reluctant Learner the incentive to complete their qualification.

Accommodating employers can move a Learner from a work place where the Learner would not be carrying out the full range of work, to a new location where the Learner is able to carry out the tasks that need to be assessed.

An employer can also provide evidence by way of documents completed by the Learner, Witness Testimony and references.

Clients

Clients and Customers are able to provide an insight into a Learner's performance from a different perspective.
The Client/Customer can provide Witness Testimonies to enable you to fill unique source of evidence.
gaps in the evidence you have gathered by other means..

The Assessor

The role of the assessor is much more than merely assessing a Learner against a set of criteria. Your role includes being diplomatic to the Learner's employer, supervisor colleagues and clients, because you need their help to complete your Learner's qualification as easily as possible. To do this use your knowledge of the qualification to see where you can easily gather evidence and identify any shortfalls, you will then be able to organise the other members of the assessment team to gather the required evidence for you.

Another role is that of Motivator, it is your job to motivate the rest of the team to gather the required evidence for you.
Most Learners respond well when given positive feedback and can easily visualise how they can achieve their goal.

The assessor role is the simple part of job. Has the Learner demonstrated competence of the relevant criteria?

The assessor also needs to maintain records of the assessment process, this is not only a requirement of Standard 9, but also any lost records will disadvantage the Learner and you will have to carry out further assessments to prove the competence of your Learner.

Another role for the assessor is that of internal quality assurance. Make sure your work complies with all the requirements of your centre's quality assurance team and the outcomes of Standardisation Meetings. If your work passes the scrutiny of the quality assurance process you will make both your life and that of the internal quality assurance team easier and less stressful.

Key Points

Encourage the Assessment to gather evidence for you, this will make your life easier and more productive.

The Assessment Team consists of anyone who can gather evidence that is reliable and authentic and includes;

The Learner, their Colleagues, their Supervisor, their Employer, Clients and You, their Assessor

Why Carry-out an Assessment Visit?

Before you read any further, consider the question, 'Why do I carry out on site assessment visits?'

Your reasons could include; 'to carry out an observation', 'to maintain contact with the Learner', 'to complete the Learner's documentation', and 'to provide the Learner with support' etc.

As far as this book is concerned there are only two objectives of an assessment visit;

1   To gather sufficient evidence to deem a Learner competent.
2   To promote the assessment centre or college and recruit more Learners.

If you are unable to gather sufficient evidence to deem the Learner competent, find ways for the Learner to gather the required Evidence for you, remember you can use colleagues, the supervisor, employer and clients etc. to provide evidence. Giving good feedback will inspire the Learner to get the required evidence for you.

Find potential Learners for your centre by talking to the Learners' co-workers and management. Raise the profile of your centre by handing out business cards, leave flyers on the tables in the canteen, and put a notice on the canteen notice board. Always present a professional image.

Key Points

The aim of an assessment visit is to gather sufficient evidence to deem a Learner competent.

Assessment Visits are a valuable resource for recruiting new Learners.

Finding Learners for other Assessors should be a reciprocal arrangement for the benefit of all assessors within your college or training centre.

Assessing Different Levels of NVQ

The different Levels of NVQ's reflect the different roles and responsibilities of the Learners.

Level 1 Learners are told what to do.
Level 2 Learners can work on their own.
Level 3 Learners supervise Level 1 & 2 workers.
Level 4 and above Learners have a higher overall responsibility including supervising Level 1, 2 & 3 workers.

As you would expect, Learners undertaking different Levels of qualification require different levels of support, however, given appropriate encouragement and guidance, they **can all gather evidence for you.**

If you give Level 3 Learners a 'wish list' they should be able to gather most of their evidence for you.

Enrolment & Induction; the Big Opportunity

Enrolment and Induction are essential tools, allowing you to filter out inappropriate Learners.

Before you do anything else, carry out an Initial Assessment.
A thorough Initial Assessment can save time in two ways.

1   Avoiding signing up inappropriate Learners
2   Identifying prior qualifications that could be counted towards a qualification.

Inappropriate Learners.
Enrolment of inappropriate Learners will;
1   waste your time,
2   waste your college / centre's time
3   cost money (registrations, portfolios etc.)
4   withdrawn Learners will spoil your achievement statistics
5   poor achievement statistics will affect future funding.

You need to be sure that the Learner has the required level of occupational competence.

On more than one occasion I have had a labourer hoping to gain a Level 2 bricklayer qualification, by 'jumping on the line', and trying to pull the wool over my eyes. Be aware and speak to the Learner's supervisor to confirm that the Learner is working in the correct role.

If you have any suspicions return a little while after your visit to see if the Learner is still carrying out the work.

You also need to assess the Learners' numeracy and literacy skills to make sure the Learner will be able to complete the qualification and be eligible for funding.

A Learner's literacy skills will have an effect on their completion of the knowledge requirement of their qualification.

Problems such as dyslexia can be overcome by asking the knowledge questions verbally and recording the answers on a digital recorder.

An Awarding Body may require assessments to be conducted in English (or Gaelic). If this is the case, the Learner's language skills will need to be assessed.

Last year an assessor signed up a Learner from an Eastern European country without checking his language skills. When the Learner came to complete his job knowledge it became obvious that he did not have the language skills required by the Awarding Body.

The Learner had to be withdrawn (lowering our timely completion statistics). He was legitimately very angry to be withdrawn and threatened legal action citing discrimination. This could have had a negative impact on our reputation.

Enrolling unsuitable Learners wastes the Learners time and their displeasure could have a disastrous effect on your centre's reputation and ability to recruit future Learners.

The Skill Scan is an essential tool to check that the Learner is working towards the correct qualification and able to produce the required evidence for the qualification. Your learner may not be fully aware of the requirements.

Discussing the contents of each Unit and how the criteria can be evidenced ensures the Learner is not only aware of the requirements but, actively involved in planning their assessment.

Prior Learning / Qualifications.
If your Learner can provide evidence of their numeracy and literacy skills they may not be required to complete a numeracy and literacy test (check with your manager). This could save you time during enrolment.

If a Learner can provide evidence of previously achieved qualifications, Units may be counted towards the current qualification. This can occur when a Learner progresses from a Level 2 qualification to a Level 3.

Check with your quality assurance team that the Units in the Level 2 qualification have not changed and can be used.

At induction / enrolment the Learner is at their most enthusiastic. Make the most of their eagerness.

Discuss the various assessment methods and explain how the Learner can gather evidence for you. For instance, you can encourage the Learner to ask their colleagues to take photos and videos of the work (when appropriate) and to supply the witness' contact details so you can authenticate the evidence.

You can also ask the Learner can also get references from their employer or clients for you. It is worth giving the Learner a list of the kind of things you would like their employer or client to refer to in their reference.

Ask the Learner questions about their work.
Are there any products available to use as evidence?
Are there any witnesses willing to give testimonies?
Is the Learner carrying out any work which could be put into an observation?
Are there any documents the Learner has created or completed?

Enrolment is the perfect time to give the Learner the knowledge questions and the resources needed to complete them. Give the Learner a deadline in which to complete the questions and also your contact details so you can be contacted should the Learner have any problems.

Giving the Learner a deadline is essential as it keeps the Learner focused and provides a target to be achieved.

Phone the Learner regularly to find out if there are any problems with the questions. If there are problems, could the Learner be dyslexic and too embarrassed to admit the fact? To get over issues such as dyslexia offer to carry out the knowledge questioning verbally.

Whilst on the phone remind the Learner to take more photos, get witness testimonies and prepare for professional discussions.

It would be inappropriate to make an assessment decision before a Learner is registered, however, **enrolment is a great opportunity to gather evidence and it should not be wasted.**

Gather as much Evidence as possible.

Evidence can be written up before a Learner is registered with the Awarding Body, as long as no assessment decisions are made.

Once the Learner has been registered you can make your assessment decisions. In making your assessment decisions you will have identified any additional evidence you need to deem the Learner competent.

Inform the Learner of any additional evidence that is required as soon as possible, giving the Learner the opportunity to gather the evidence for you.
Save time and traveling by giving your feedback through the post, email or phone or via an e-portfolio.

Key Points

Filter out inappropriate Learners and identify prior qualifications.

A newly enrolled Learner is eager. Exploit your Learners' eagerness. Encourage the Learner to take possession of their qualification and gather their evidence for you.

If enrolling at the Learners' place of work, collect witness testimonies, documents and products which can be assessed when the Learner is registered. Carry out an observation.

Give the Learner the knowledge part of their qualification to complete before your next visit. Give the Learner your contact details.

The Ideal Assessment Plan

The given way of producing an assessment plan is to discuss the assessment session with the Learner and to declare; where, when and what you are going to assess and what assessment methods you intend to use.
Having a preconceived Assessment Plan massively disadvantages both you and your Learner.

An assessment plan that is created before you know what assessment opportunities might arise could prevent you from taking advantage of unexpected assessment opportunities.

An Ideal Assessment Plan	
1	**When**; My Learner will inform me of a time when I can maximise the range of assessment criteria that can be covered during my visit.
2	**What**; I will carry out holistic assessments so that I gather evidence for as many Units as possible.
3	**Assessment Methods**; I will use a range of assessment methods as appropriate.
4	**Historical Evidence;** I will aim to get historical evidence using Witness Testimonies, Employer References, Client Statements, Documentation or any other form of evidence which I deem as safe, reliable, relevant and valid.
5	**Goal;** My goal is to be able to deem the Learner competent for the qualification by the end of the assessment session.

This allows the assessor to take advantage of any unexpected opportunities which may arise.

Before carrying out any assessment, the approval of the Learner and their supervisor should be sought as it may be inappropriate to take photographic or video evidence in a sensitive environment such as a school, bank or hospital.

Key Points

Plan for the unexpected.

Make sure your assessment plan takes advantage all appropriate assessment opportunities.

Ensure your assessment plan complies with your assessment strategy.

A Dynamic Assessment Plan

To maximise the assessment opportunities use 'Dynamic Assessing' techniques. Each piece of evidence leads to another piece of evidence in a 'Domino' effect.

1   Plan the assessment to cover criteria you have identified using 'Gap Analysis'.
2   Plan questioning around the assessment to provide the supporting knowledge relevant to the work being carried out.
3   Ask the Learner to identify work carried out recently which may be used as Product Evidence
4   Ask the Learner for a witness who can authenticate the product evidence.
5   The witness can also provide a Witness Testimony (and   may be able to identify even more Products for your Learner).
6   Each Product should be discussed with the Learner thus producing several Professional Discussions.
7   Each Professional Discussion should be guided to produce evidence of both performance and knowledge.

A 'Real Life' Example of Dynamic Assessing

I recently made a planned assessment visit on a bricklayer. It was planned so that I could observe him 'setting out'. Bricklayers seldom have the opportunity to set-out a building, so I was pleased that he had contacted me to arrange the visit.

While I was observing the Learner I asked him a few questions about what he was doing and what he would do if there was a problem (I referenced this against his Knowledge Requirement). I also asked him what work he had carried out last week. He pointed out a couple of windows with arches over the top and he also pointed out a garage block he had worked on. I realised these pieces of work could be used as Product Evidence so I took photos of both 'Products'.

During the Learner's tea break I asked him how he went about erecting the arches and recorded the Professional Discussion on my digital recorder. I then asked the Learner about the garage block and recorded this Professional Discussion (this provided sufficiency in the setting out Unit). I guided both Professional Discussions to cover some of the Knowledge criteria.

I then sought out the Learner's supervisor to authenticate the Product and provide a Witness Testimony. I recorded three Witness Testimonies, one for each Product and a general one relating to the Learner's compliance with Health and Safety etc. Before I left the site, I scanned a copy of the Learner's Induction

Documentation.

The result of my visit was; the planned Observation, three sessions of Knowledge Questioning, two Products, two Professional Discussions, three Witness Testimonies and a document. I used the evidence from this, my second visit, to prove competence and sufficiency for the qualification.

If I had videoed the visit I could have referenced the whole visit with bullet points and saved myself time when referencing.

Flowchart of the Example

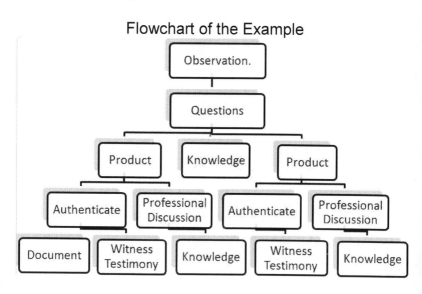

Key Points

One piece of evidence will always lead to another.

Ask the Learner questions.

Identify 'products' to be used as a basis for professional discussions.

Witnesses can identify additional Products

'Don't Stop Till You Get Enough' (Michael Jackson 1979)

Preparing for your Assessment Visit

It is vital to prepare for your assessment visit.

Planning and preparation for your assessment visit should have begun before you left your Learner on the last visit.

You should have discussed with the Learner what evidence was still required, and planned how the Learner was going to collect it for you.

Check your Learner is available to assess.

Before setting out on an assessment visit, contact the Learner or the Learner's manager to make sure the Learner is at work and available for assessment.

I once drove out to visit a Learner in the middle of Kent, only to find the Learner had decided to go to the pub to watch England play in the World Cup!, the result was a wasted a 150 mile round trip. Also check if there are any activities going on at the assessment location that could prevent you from carrying out your assessments, for instance' there may be a Royal visit (this happened to me when the Princess Royal visited a location where I had planned to carry out an assessment). It also pays to check that the Learner is carrying appropriate work. On one occasion, when I went to assess one of my bricklayer Learners he was actually laying carpet!

Are there any other Learners to assess?

Check to see if you have any other Learners to assess, either at the same location or nearby, who can be assessed on the same visit.

Check your equipment.

Make sure your mobile phone is fully charged. It can be very frustrating to arrive for an assessment, only to find that your phone has a flat battery, and you are unable to use the camera or the digital voice recorder.

Make sure you have plenty of room on memory cards etc. Without sufficient memory you will be unable to save your photos, digital voice recordings or videos.

Check your documents.

Make a 'wish list' of all the outstanding evidence. This is easily done using the Gap Analysis tool found on most e-portfolios.

Produce a template to help you steer your Professional Discussions and Witness Testimonies in the desired direction. Check you have all the documents which may need to be signed by the Learner also check that you have a set of the 'Standards' to show the Learner.

Spare Knowledge Questions.

Take a spare set of the Knowledge Questions. It is surprising how many Learners 'forget' to bring the 'completed' question sheets in to work. If necessary you can ask the Learner the questions verbally and record the answers (if you have a spare set of knowledge questions).

Spare Enrolment documents.

Take a spare set of enrolment documents in case there are new Learners to enroll. Take plenty of business cards to give to potential prospective Learners.

At the Location

Planning of the assessment should continue when you arrive at the assessment location. Your Assessment Plan should be dynamic and adaptable to take advantage of unforeseen opportunities.

Ask your Learner what work has been carried out since your last visit. You may discover a whole range of work that the Learner has considered unimportant and not worth mentioning, which could provide valuable evidence. Plan with your Learner how you can assess any additional evidence.

Key Points

Phone your Learners to check that the assessment can go ahead and check if there other learners working nearby who can be assessed at the same time.

Check you have the documentation you need.

Check your equipment, batteries etc

Assessment Methods

There are a wide variety of assessment methods available to the assessor; ultimately they all have the same goal, to demonstrate the Learner's competence and knowledge.

There are three types of Assessment Method, Direct, Indirect and Remote.

Direct Assessment Methods.
Direct Assessments are made by the assessor carrying out direct assessments of the Learner.

Direct assessment include assessment methods such as Observation of the Learner, Videos created by the assessor, Documents gathered by the assessor and Written or Verbal Questioning by the assessor.

Indirect Assessment Methods.
Indirect Assessment is the assessment of evidence provided by a third party.

Examples of Indirect Assessment include Witness Testimonies, Employer References, and Client Statements etc.

Remote Assessment Methods
Remote Assessment makes the most of both Direct and Indirect Assessment Methods, allowing assessment to take place without visiting the Learners' place of work.

Direct Assessment may be gathered remotely using methods such as Professional Discussions and Knowledge Questions taken over the 'phone and recorded or via video conferencing over the internet.

Indirect Assessment can also be gathered remotely. Evidence such as photos produced by the Learner can be posted or emailed to the assessor. The evidence can be then authenticated over the phone or by post etc. Videos can be filmed by a work colleague and emailed to the assessor. Witness Testimonies can be taken over the phone and digitally recorded and loaded onto the portfolio.

For more information see 'The Virtual Visit'

Key Points

The key to successful and efficient assessment is to make the most of Direct, Indirect and Remote Assessment Methods.

Prior Learning and Experience

Prior learning and experience should be identified during the induction and enrolment process.

Many qualifications include Units from other qualifications the Learner may have achieved. These can usually be excluded from assessment, however qualifications change over time so it would expedient to check with your quality assurance team that they are still current and applicable.

Key Points

Identify any prior learning and experience at enrolment.

Check with your quality assurance team that previously gained qualifications can be counted towards the current qualification.

Observation

An Observation of the Learner at work is the best evidence any assessor or quality assurance professional can hope for. Use a holistic approach to your Observation identifying evidence that can be used across Units. This will maximise the effectiveness of your assessments.

To get the most out of an Observation don't just look, but listen as well. How does the Learner interact with others? Do these interactions provide evidence of competence, and do they convey knowledge that can be referenced?

During the Observation ask questions about the work or work environment, this helps the Learner to relate the knowledge questions to the real world.
Ask the Learner about work carried out in the past. This encourages the Learner to take ownership of the qualification and encourages the Learner to identify work which may be used as Product Evidence. Product Evidence can then be used as a basis of a Professional Discussion.

Products should be photographed and authenticated. While the Learner's witness is authenticating the evidence you can ask questions about how the Learner carried out the work, thereby gaining a Witness Testimony.

Take photos of the Observation, these can be used to

support your observation, but more importantly, they act as aide memoir when writing up your assessments. They can also be used to illustrate your Observation for the benefit of the quality assurance team. Supporting photos are easily uploaded onto an e-portfolio where they can be viewed whilst writing up and referencing the Observation Report.

Key Points

Ask questions relating to the work being carried out during an Observation .

Ask about work carried out in the past (to identify possible 'products'.

Ensure your Observation is holistic in nature, covering as wide a range of criteria for as many Units as possible.

Video

Video is a highly efficient and versatile Assessment Method. Videos can be produced by the assessor or the Learner's colleagues. Anyone can easily produce a video using a 'smart' phone, digital camera or video camera. The video does not need to be the length of a feature film, short clips can demonstrate competence and are quicker to reference and quality assure.

One of the advantages of using video is that it can include sound (great for recording answers to questions or information from reliable witnesses).
Another is its ability to zoom in; this allows the assessor to stand at a safe distance from the activity being recorded.

Another great advantage of video evidence is that it can be produced by a colleague of the Learner. The Learner can then send the video clip to the assessor who can reference the evidence in the comfort of the office, saving the assessor the time and expense of traveling to the Learner.

Another advantage of using video evidence is that it can be referenced using 'bullet points', this saves the time writing up a long report.

Finally Video Evidence also allows the quality assurance team to actually see the Learner at work.

There are two things you should be aware of.

The first is that video tells 'the truth, the whole truth and nothing but the truth'.

Some time ago I watched a video of a Learner guiding a crane which was lowering a large steel girder. Unfortunately the Learner was about 100 foot above the ground and standing on another girder without a safety harness. Not only did it show the Learner was not competent, it also showed that the assessor was not concerned about health and safety.

The second thing to be aware of is; it is not always appropriate to video evidence.

In some establishments (such as hospitals, care homes, children's homes, prisons, banks etc.) producing a video would be inappropriate. You should check with the supervisor and the Learner's colleagues and clients etc. before starting filming.

Video Evidence can quickly and easily be loaded into e-portfolios. The Intelligent Portfolio from Hedgehog Solutions Ltd. allows the Time Stamping of video evidence; this allows the assessor, quality assurance team and centre manager to quickly identify specific parts of the video where criteria have been referenced.

Key Points

Video clips are easy to produce and quick to reference.

Check it is OK to use video at the assessment location (it is not acceptable for security or confidentiality issues in banks, schools, hospitals and military bases etc.).

Ask Learner to enlist the help of a colleague to record the Learner at work.

View my Youtube demonstration 'Referencing and Quality Assuring Video Evidence'. (http://www.youtube.com/watch ?v=YCFNmtKADXs).

Professional Discussion

Professional Discussions are a great way of obtaining evidence for activities which are rarely carried out, however they do require planning.

A good place to start is to get the Learner to identify prior work and obtain photos if possible (photos help the Learner focus and recall each step of an operation).

The Learner also needs to supply the contact details of a witness (such as a colleague, client or supervisor) who can authenticate the work referred to in the Professional Discussion.

Next you need a plan, as you will have to guide the Learner to cover the points you need to cover. A Professional Discussion Template should be produced.

To get the most of a Professional Discussion ensure you are in a quiet location where you will not be disturbed.

It is often a good idea to ask the Learner to describe each step of the operation being discussed as if you knew nothing about it.

Guide the discussion using your Professional Discussion Template and be careful not ask questions that can be answer with a 'yes' or a 'no', instead ask the Learner to 'how did you?'

One of the most important things to remember is to LISTEN to the Learner; if the Learner says he did something ask how, ask about health and safety issues etc. Guide the Learner to discussing how they got over any problems or health & safety issues.

A well planned Professional Discussion can cover a vast amount of performance criteria as well as demonstrating the Learner's knowledge.

A great feature of the Professional Discussion is that it can be carried-out over the phone, thereby saving you time traveling to and from the Learner's workplace. A simple adapter can be purchased online to record your Professional Discussion, which can then be uploaded onto the portfolio.

It is quick and easy to load and reference audio evidence using an e-portfolio. The Intelligent Portfolio allows you to 'Time Stamp' the Professional Discussion, speeding up the quality assurance process.

Key Points

Preparation is key.

Ask your Learner to prepare by obtaining a photo to form the basis of the Professional Discussion.

Prepare a Professional Discussion Template.

Check your Digital Recorder has fresh batteries (take spares).

Check there is plenty of room on your memory card.

Find a quiet location for the Discussion

Professional Discussion Template

Professional Discussions can be a great assessment method, especially if you are prepared with a good Professional Discussion Template.

The template should be used to guide the discussion allowing the Learner to explain how they carried out their work. A good template should steer the discussion over each stage of the operation, providing evidence for a range of Units.

The areas to be covered might include;
1   interpreting information,
2   selecting resources,
3   preparation,
4   carrying out the task,
5   health & safety aspects,
6   protecting the work and surrounding area,
7   clearing up and disposal of waste.

Professional Discussion Template Example

Begin with an introduction e.g. Assessor Name Learner Name Date, We are discussing work carried out by the Learner
Where and when was this work carried out?
What information were you given about the requirements of the work you carried out?
What preparation did you carry out?
How did you carry out the task?
Were there any special features?
What resources did you use?
Were there any hazards with the resources you used?
How do you know about these hazards?
How did you protect yourself from these hazards?
Did you have to protect your work or the surrounding area?

Witness Testimony

Witness Testimonies are an essential part of the assessor's tool-kit. An assessor cannot observe a learner each and every day and will probably be unable to directly observe a Learner carrying out certain duties.

The Learner's supervisor is well placed to provide a Witness Testimony describing the work the Learner has undertaken. Customers and Clients are able to provide a wide range of evidence often covering criteria a supervisor would not witness. Colleagues of the Learner may be able to provide witness testimonies of work carried out in the past during previous employments.

An advantage of using witness testimonies is that, as well as being taken during an assessment visit they can also be taken over the phone and recorded.

Make sure you have the witnesses' contact details and credentials before recording the witness testimony.

It is essential to prepare for a witness testimony to guide the conversation to cover the criteria you require evidence to cover.

Create a Template for each Witness. The Client and Employer testimonies would have a very different content to that of the Supervisor.

Avoid falling into the habit of asking direct or leading questions. Approach questions from another angle, for instance questions such as 'Does the Learner...? Could be asked as 'what would be the consequences if the Learner failed to.....?' From the response you may be able to infer compliance.

When taking a Witness Testimony it is important to LISTEN. The witness can bring to light work carried out previously, and this could provide evidence to cover an even wider range of criteria than originally anticipated.

Make a note of the activities identified by the witness and consider their use as a basis for a Professional Discussion.

Remember a Witness Testimony can be as brief or as long as you like. Even the briefest discussion with a supervisor or work colleague can provide essential evidence to cover difficult to observe criteria.

Witness Testimonies are easy to load into an e-portfolio and the referenced criteria can be 'Time Stamped' to enable quick and easy quality assurance.

Key Points

Preparation is essential to make the most of a Witness Testimony.

Create a Witness Testimony Template.

Include the date, the Learners' name, the qualification, the location, the witness' name, position and contact details.

Save traveling to the assessment venue by conducting a Witness Testimony over the phone.

Can the Witness provide a testimony for your other

Witness Testimony Template

Creating a template for your Witness Testimonies avoids wasted opportunities and ensures the witness is guided to the criteria you need the witness to cover.

It is worth keeping the template short and succinct as the witness may not have much time to talk and seeing a long list of criteria may deter the witness from giving you their valuable time.

Work through your Standards to identify any criteria that may be difficult to obtain using assessment methods such as Observation. Some criteria such as; 'completion of the work within the allotted time' can only be demonstrated by a witness who knows both the allotted time and whether or not the Learner completes the work within the allotted time.

Similarly criteria such as 'complies with information from inductions can only be confirmed by someone who knows both the induction information and whether or not the Learner complies with the information.

The example on the following page can be discussed with the witness within a couple of minutes.

It is quite easy to encourage a more talkative supervisor to give you an in depth description of the work carried out by the Learner.

Witness Testimony Template Example

Can you give me your name and contact details? (this will provide an audit trail)
How long has the Learner been working with you? (if the learner has been working for a while they must be working to the required standard)
Has the Learner been inducted? (completion of documentation)
What was covered in the induction? (range of information)
What would happen if the Learner failed to comply with the information given at induction (compliance with range of health and safety rules)
What work has the Learner carried out since working with you? (range of performance criteria)
What happens if the Learner fails to complete the work within the allotted time?   (completion of work within allotted time)
How does the Learner protect the work and surrounding area? (an assessor may not personally observe the Learner protecting of the work)
Where does the Learner store their tools/equipment/personal protective equipment? (storage may not be observed)
Does the Learner have to lift any heavy equipment etc.? (lifting may only be done on rare occasions)
How does the Learner lift heavy articles? (kinetic lifting)

Key Points

Produce a template to help you to guide the witness testimony to cover the required criteria.

Reduce the Template to key-words as reading questions from a prompt will disturb the natural flow of the witness testimony.

Tick off key words as you cover the criteria.

Knowledge Questioning

Preparation
Before asking any questions it is a good idea to work through the questions to see if any are repeated from other Units. If the questions are repeated you may be able to infer the knowledge across Units.

Care should be taken when cross referencing, as some repeated questions may refer to activities specific to certain Units. If this is the case you may be able to expand a question to include elements from more than one criteria or Unit. This will reduce the overall number of questions to be answered, which will reduce a Learner's apprehension.

A cross-referenced question sheet will save you, and the Learner, a great deal of time. Take a look at the example on the following page.

Engagement
Encourage the Learner to complete the knowledge part of the qualification as soon as possible. The longer the delay in completing the knowledge, the more reluctant a Learner may become to completing the questions.

This will also help you identify if there is a problem. If a Learner finds any excuse not to produce their completed knowledge questions there could be a reason that needs to be addressed before it becomes an issue. A Learner that fails to complete their knowledge will ultimately have to be withdrawn having a serious impact on effect on your 'timely completions'.

Every Learner is Different.

Some Learners are fine writing answers to questions on a Question and Answer sheet.

Mature Learners who left school many years ago will not have had to complete a bank of questions for years and may be nervous at the prospect of having their knowledge questioned.

Some Learners may lack certain literacy skills and some may be slow writers. Others may have other 'more important' things to do.

Fortunately there are ways to overcome these issues.

The Solution;

The assessor can read the questions and scribe the answers for the Learner (this is very time consuming as each answer should be written down verbatim, and the process must be declared on the answer sheet and the declaration signed).

Another way is for the assessor to read the questions and the Learner answer verbally and with his responses recorded digitally. This is by far the best solution. Audio tracks can be quickly uploaded onto an e-portfolio and time stamped during referencing.

If you are reading the questions, make sure the Learner cannot see the questions or the Learner will try to read them and this will slow the whole process down.

Best Practice

By far the best way to obtain evidence for the knowledge requirement is to ask questions during an assessment.

Observations are ideal situations to ask questions, the questions can be made relevant to the work being carried out.

Asking questions such as, "Do you ever get incorrect instructions? and "how did you get over them?" or, "'Do you ever find defects with your tools or materials?" can help the Learner relate the knowledge requirement to the real world of work.

Recording Observations and questions on a digital voice recorder allows for very quick referencing of both the performance and the knowledge criteria.

Knowledge from Other Sources

Professional Discussions can easily be guided to cover many of the knowledge requirements.

Ask the Learner "why did you", or "were there any problems" and "how did you get over them" during the discussion.

It is important to record the answers and to reference them against the knowledge requirement.

Key Points

Create a cross-referenced question sheet.

Prepare your Learner for their knowledge at enrollment and complete their knowledge questions as soon as possible.

Look out for Learner that may have problems with reading or writing, offer them the option of completing their questions verbally.

Reference knowledge that is demonstrated during professional discussions etc.

Cross Referenced Question Sheet

A cross-referenced question sheet saves everyone's time and can help you avoid asking the same question twice.

A cross -referenced question sheet also makes quality assurance easier.

Quest No.	Unit 1	Unit 2	Unit 3	Unit 4	Unit 5	Unit 6	Knowledge Requirement
1	3.2		4.2	4.2	4.2	4.2	What PPE do you wear and why?
2	3.3		4.3	4.3	4.3	4.3	What should you do if there is a problem with your PPE
3	3.4						Where do you store your PPE?
4	4.1			1.1	1.1	1.1	When do you receive health and safety information?
5			3.2				What problems could you have with the equipment you use?

Quest No.	Unit 1	Unit 2	Unit 3	Unit 4	Unit 5	Unit 6	Knowledge Requirement
6		1.1	3.3	3.3	3.3	3.3	How do you report problems with the equipment you use?
7		2.1					How do you plan your work?
8		3.1					How do you receive the information you need to carry out your work?
9		1.1		7.2	7.2	7.2	How do you report problems with the information you are given?

Where appropriate, the questions have been cross referenced to more than one Unit.

Key Points

A cross-referenced question sheet reduces the number of questions the Learner must answer.

A cross-referenced question sheet saves time and simplifies the quality assurance process.

Product Evidence

Products are a great way to gather historical evidence. Products can cover a wide range of Units and are quick and easy to reference. A Product can be any piece of work produced by the Learner, the work can take any form, however it must be authenticated.

During a visit ask the Learner, or their supervisor, what work they carried out yesterday, last week or even last year. If the product provides additional useful evidence and can be authenticated, use it.

A quick and efficient way of referencing a Product is for the assessor takes a photograph of the Product and reference the criteria covered. Photos or scanned images are easily uploaded, written descriptions can be entered into a report and a verbal description uploaded as an audio track.

A Learner can also easily produce his own Product Evidence by taking photos of his work and giving you the contact details of a reliable witness to authenticate the evidence. Remember, authentication can be carried out over the phone. Ask the witness if it O.K. to record the conversation.

Whilst on the phone authenticating the product evidence, the witness may be able to give you a witness testimony to cover other criteria which is still outstanding.

It is essential to check what evidence still needs to be gathered, before phoning the witness to authenticate the Product. This will give you the opportunity to ask the witness if they have witnessed the Learner demonstrating competence of the missing criteria.

Checking which criteria requires more evidence is easily done by using Gap Analysis on e-portfolios.

Remember to record the witness' contact details to provide an audit trail for the quality assurance team.

Products are a perfect basis on which to build a Professional Discussion, especially if your Learner has provided photos

Key Points

All Products must be authenticated this provides the assessor with an ideal opportunity to obtain a Witness Testimony.

Products can form the basis of a Professional Discussion.

Inference

Inference is a legitimate and vital assessment method, which is often under-used.
An e-portfolio will allow you to quickly flick from Unit to Unit. You can easily identify criteria which are repeated.

Criteria in one Unit is often repeated in another Unit and the competence may be legitimately inferred from one Unit to another.

You can also use repeated criteria to provide sufficiency of evidence.

When inferring, you should always explain your rationale for using inference.

It is our responsibility, as assessors, to check if competence can be inferred from one Unit to another
Not inferring competence when appropriate can seriously disadvantage your Learners.

Key Points
Inference is a legitimate assessment method.

Infer competence and sufficiency.

Have a standardisation meeting to discuss inference.

The Assessment Visit

An Assessment Visit is made up of three components; Arrival, Assessment, and Leaving. Each component needs to be carefully considered to maximise the productivity of the Visit.

Key Points

There are three keys to an efficient and successful assessment visit.

The first is a thorough knowledge of the criteria within the various Units of the qualification.

The second is to thoroughly prepare for the visit

The third key is the ability to grasp every assessment opportunity and employ a wide range of assessment methods.

Arrival

There are several documents you should have with you when you arrive at the assessment venue.

The first is a 'wish list' of evidence you need to prove the Learner competent.
The second document is a Witness Testimony Template to guide the Learner's supervisor to give you a useful and meaningful Witness Testimony.
The third document is a prompt sheet to steer a Professional Discussion to cover the points you have identified in your 'wish list'
.

Gathering evidence should start before you even meet the Learner.
When entering the assessment venue take a look around and note if there are any health and safety signs, warning signs or prohibitions. When you meet your Learner you will be able confirm that the Learner is complying with the rules and signage.

Make a note of any security procedures; is there a signing in book? Has the Learner signed in? If yes, make a copy, you now have documentary evidence.

You have now gathered evidence before you have even met the Learner!

If you need to be inducted, ask for a copy of the Induction Checklist, you will then be able to assess whether your Learner is complying with the induction rules and procedures. You can ask the person inducting you if your Learner complies with the rules. If your Learner does comply, ask the inductor if they would mind being a witness, and get their contact details to provide an audit trail.

Ask for a copy of your Learner's induction documentation, this will provide you with evidence that the Learner completes relevant documentation.

The Learner's supervisor is a vital source of information and is able to authenticate evidence. It is essential that you keep the Learner's supervisor 'on board'.

At your first meeting with the Learner's Supervisor ask for their contact details (this could allow you to take a Witness Testimony over the phone at a later date).

Explain to the supervisor how important their input is and discuss the possibility of them providing a Witness Testimony. They may also be able to identify work the Learner has carried out that could be used as Product Evidence.

Additional Learners
Check with the supervisor if any other workers need their qualifications. On a recent visit to Milton Keynes one of the two Learners due to be enrolled was not on site that day, however, the supervisor identified another worker who needed his NVQ, the second Learner made the visit financially viable.

Key Points

Prepare a 'wish list' of criteria to be covered.

Check you have all the documents your Learner may need to sign (e.g. Candidate Contact) and the Supervisor's contact details (this enables you to phone the supervisor for a witness testimony later).

The supervisor may be able to identify suitable prospective Learners for you.

Assessment

The Learner

Put your Learner at ease, the Learner may be embarrassed talking in front of colleagues. Take your Learner to one side to ensure confidentiality while you discuss their progress etc. this is especially true if they have problems with numeracy or literacy.

Outstanding Evidence

Use your Aide Memoir to ascertain what evidence you need. Discuss the required evidence with your Learner and plan how to best gather the required evidence.

If the Learner is not going to produce the required evidence through Observation, consider what other assessment methods available to you.

What work has the Learner carried out recently? Are there any Products that can be assessed and can they be authenticated? What work has the Learner carried out in the past? Could this be used as a basis for a professional discussion?

Witnesses

Can the Learner supply a witness who can provide a Witness Testimony or authenticate the Professional Discussion? Remember witnesses need not be the supervisor; the witness could be a colleague or a client.

Holistic Assessment

Assessment should be holistic and cover as wide a range of Units as possible.

It is extremely rare that a Unit is completely 'stand alone' and not relate to other Units. Look at your Standards to see how the Units relate and if the same criteria is repeated in more than one Unit can it be inferred from one Unit to another.

Ask questions

Whilst carrying out an assessment ask the Learner questions. Relating the knowledge questions to the work being carried out encourages the Learner to give relevant answers.

Ask the Learner about work carried out in your absence. This can help identify potential Products on which you can base Professional Discussions.

Ask the Learner's supervisor to identify Products and to supply Witness Testimonies.

Key Points

Assess holistically

Encourage the Learner and their supervisor to identify suitable Product Evidence.

Use a wide range of assessment methods.

Ask the Learner and supervisor questions.

Leaving

Missing Evidence

Before leaving the assessment venue it is essential to check your 'wish list'. Have you have covered all the evidence you set out to gather?

Consider the consequences of not gathering all the available evidence, perhaps another visit, wasting valuable time and expense.

Take a good look at your assessment 'wish list' and identify any additional evidence that can be gathered on the day, rather than returning for another visit.

The Knowledge Requirement

Has the Learner completed their knowledge questions? If not, why not? Has the Learner got all the information they need to complete the knowledge?

Sometimes a Learner may 'forget' their knowledge questions; this could be due to them having 'more important' things to do. It may also be an indication that they are dyslexic and need help.

If they have failed to produce their knowledge, there is a reason. Sit down with them somewhere quiet and work through the requirement with them.
Remember you can scribe the answers for them if they are dyslexic or you can ask the questions verbally and record the answers on a digital recorder.

Planning the Next Visit

Revisit your 'Assessment Wish List' and discuss with your Learner the outstanding criteria. Plan how your Learner can gather the required evidence for you.

Arrange for your Learner to produce Product Photos, Videos, Witness Testimonies, Client Statements, Employer References and Professional Discussions. These can all be sent to you by email, text, phone or uploaded onto an e-portfolio via the Learner Portal.

Learner Feedback
This stage of the visit is vital in keeping your Learner 'on track'. Giving good feedback is essential to keep your Learner enthused and looking for opportunities to gather evidence for you.
Make the most of the opportunity by making sure the Learner knows exactly what evidence you need and how to gather the evidence for you.

Before leaving

Take a look at your assessment visit checklist. Have you got sufficient evidence? If you cannot deem your Learner competent with the evidence you have, consider are there are there any additional assessment methods that you can use before leaving.

Make sure you have the Learner Contact Record and the Reviews etc. signed.

Ensure you have Witness' contact details. Check what time would be convenient to phone them to conduct a

Witness Testimony over the phone, should you need it.

Make sure the Learner has your contact details. Remind your Learner to contact if they have any problems or concerns or if they are going away on holiday.

Finally, check the Learner's contact details are still valid.

Key Points

Do you have sufficient evidence to deem the Learner competent?

Has the Learner agreed to a strategy to collect the outstanding evidence for you?

Are there any new Learners?

Put a notice up in the canteen informing other potential Learners of the qualifications your college or centre delivers.

Hand out your business cards.

The Virtual Visit

Why travel for hours when you can gather evidence remotely?

We are now well into the 21st Century and technology is rapidly evolving.

Mobile phones can take photos, record videos and audio and can send and receive text messages. All kinds of files can be attached to emails

Mobile devices have more and more functions, tablets, laptops and computers are commonplace and have opened up a whole new world of communications and social media is used by ever increasing numbers of people.

We must embrace these new technologies and use them to our advantage. The benefits of a Virtual Visit are enormous.

The environment;
The effect on the environment of traveling from site to site to assess learners adds to the catastrophic impact man is having on the planet.
Every time we travel to an assessment venue we contribute to the pollution which is the cause of global warming. The consumption of fossil fuels depletes the Earth's resources, resulting in ever more environmentally damaging extraction techniques, risking the ecology of vast swathes of wilderness.

Adopting the practice conducting virtual visits, whenever possible, lessens your environmental footprint, reduces pollution, conserves fossil fuels and helps to relieve traffic congestion.

Time;
The hours wasted sitting in traffic whilst traveling to and from assessment venues can be used much more productively in the office.

Financial;
The cost in relation to the time wasted whilst traveling, together with the cost of fuel and vehicle maintenance is a high proportion of the expenses incurred during the on-site assessment of workplace training.

Resources
When working from home or in the office you have all the resources you need close at hand.

Key Points

A 'Virtual Visit' will save you the time, expense and stress of travelling to and from the Learner's place of work.

Use a range of technology to gather evidence remotely.

A Virtual Visit' will reduce the amount of evidence you have to produce during an actual visit.

The Internet

The internet is a perfect platform for the 'Virtual Visit'.

Video Conferencing

If your Learner has access to the internet, online video conferencing provides a perfect medium for assessments. Platforms such as 'Skype' and 'Google+' allow you to talk face to face with your Learners with the added benefit of not having to leave your office (or even your home).

On-line video conferencing can be used for a wide range of assessment methods including; Observations, Professional Discussions and answering the Knowledge requirement. Learners can show you 'Products' they have created, they can even show you their work environment and how they work by simply moving the web cam around their workplace.

The Learner can get a supervisor or colleague to join the conversation and give a Witness Testimony. The conference can easily be recorded using screen grab technology.

The 'Cloud'

The 'Cloud' is the name given to web based storage and sharing of files etc. 'Bluetooth' technology and the use of portable memory devices such as memory cards or sticks is a convenient way for the Learner to give you digital evidence, however the 'Cloud' is by far the most convenient.

Programs such as 'Dropbox'

(https://www.dropbox.com) allow you to 'share' a folder with your Learner, your Learner can then drop files into your 'Dropbox' folder and you can view or save them into your e-portfolio. You can also drop documents such as question sheets or Reviews into the Learner's Dropbox folder.

Social Media

Many people use Social Media sites such as Facebook and YouTube. If your Learner is already using Social Media, ask them how they can pass on evidence to you using their current Social Media platform. They may be able to post their evidence onto their 'pages' for you to view.

Consider setting up a 'page' where Learners can post their evidence for you.

Many Social Media platforms have instant messaging, this is an ideal medium for sending confidential information.

Key Points

Assess Learners working in an office environment via the internet using 'video conferencing'.

Share documents via the 'cloud' or using social media.

See if your Learners currently use Social Media.

Use Social Media platforms to 'post' evidence.

Communicate your Learners via instant messaging.

Emails

Emails are a quick and convenient way of communicating with your learner, especially if they are working in an office environment. Emails can be sent and received on computers, tablets and smart phones.

A great thing about emails is that you can configure the settings to request an acknowledgment of when the Learner receives their e-mail thus maintaining an audit trail.

In situations where the Learner is prevented from using a mobile phone, emails can be the best way of communicating. Emails can be read and responded to at any time of the day or night.

Emails can be employed for a wide range of uses;
You can arrange a visit or 'virtual visit' or request evidence from a Learner or Witness. A witness can authenticate a Learner's work or give a witness testimony via email.

Also, a range of evidence etc. can be attached to emails;
Learners can attach photos of 'Products' and describe them in the body of the email (including giving you witness' contact details).
Scanned documents and brief video clips can also be attached and employers can attach references etc. to emails.

Key Points

Always get the Learner's email address at enrolment.

Email is effective for communicating with Learners working in an office environment

If the Learner changes their phone, their email may be your only point of contact.

Emails provide an audit trail.

Evidence can be attached to emails.

Mobile Phones

It is a long time since mobile phones could only be used for phone calls. They can now take photos, record videos, be used as digital voice recorders audio and be used for text messages.

The mobile phone can be a useful tool to enable you to keep in touch with your Learner. Keeping in regular touch with your Learners will keep them motivated.

Sometimes a Learner will be unable to use their mobile phone whilst at work. This could be due to the nature of the work, safety or security reasons or simply not having a 'signal'. If this is the case, simply send the Learner a text and ask the Learner to phone you back when they are able.

Recording phone calls

A phone call from a land line to a mobile phone can easily be recorded using an inexpensive device readily available over the internet.

This makes the mobile phone an ideal solution to obtaining Witness Testimonies from witnesses who may have moved on since working with the Learner.

Professional Discussions can also be carried out over the mobile phone and job knowledge questions can be asked.

Always seek permission to record the conversation.

A Learner can easily take photos of Products and send them as a picture message together with an explanationary text to the assessor.

A colleague of the Learner can take photos or even shoot a video of the Learner at work. Photos and videos of the Learner carrying out their naturally occurring duties make excellent evidence and allow the assessor and the quality assurance team to see how the Learner actually works.

Photos and videos should be accompanied by description giving as much information as possible about the work being carried out including; the date, location and witness details.

Photos and videos can be transferred to the assessor's mobile phone via blue-tooth.

Key Points

Keep in touch with your Learners via their mobile phone and keep them engaged.

The Learner can easily gather evidence for you by taking asking a colleague to take photos or shoot videos of the Learner at work.

Professional discussions and witness testimonies taken via mobile phones can be recorded using a device fitted to your landline.

Text Messaging

Texting is a very efficient way of communicating. A learner may not be able to use a mobile phone in the work place but will be able to view any text messages during breaks or after work.

A major drawback with text messaging is that it does not leave an audit trail, although they can be viewed, sent and received messages cannot be recorded (this is true today, but in the rapidly evolving world of mobile communications this could well change by tomorrow!).

An advantage of the text message is that it doesn't need to be answered when it is sent, it remains on the mobile and can be read at a convenient time. This allows the Learner to respond in their own time.

A text message can remind a Learner to send you their completed Knowledge Question Sheets or evidence.

Text messages can be used to ask the Learner to make contact or to arrange a 'Virtual Visit'.

Regular text messages can help keep the Learner engaged and an engaged Learner will help you prove their competence.

Key Points

If a Learner is unable to answer a phone call, you can send a text message to ask the Learner to call you or text to arrange a visit.

Remember text messages do not leave an audit trail.

The Telephone

The telephone is one of the most convenient assessment tools available for the Virtual Visit.

Prearrange the remote assessment with the Learner before phoning. Make sure the Learner will be in a quiet location and will have sufficient time to fully cover all the areas you wish to visit without being rushed or disturbed.

Prepare the Learner so they know exactly what you intend to cover in the phone call.

Telephone recorders are widely available on the internet and enable the recording of telephone conversations.

Make sure you ask the Learner for their permission to record the conversation.

Make sure you have your recorder prepared and you have all the information you need at your finger-tips. Ensure you have a pen and paper at hand to take notes.

Turn the recorder on!

Professional Discussions

Professional Discussions can easily be held over the phone. Be prepared, have your Professional Discussion Template and any photos the Learner has supplied in front of you before phoning.

Take your time. If you have prepared your Learner there will be no need to hurry. Tick off the points as you cover them.

Job Knowledge Questions

Asking a complete set of knowledge questions may take up a great deal of time, however if the Learner is having problems in understanding some of the questions, a quick phone call can quickly and easily alleviate any problems, thus allowing the Learner to complete their job knowledge questions.

Witness Testimonies

Why drive to see the witness when you can record a statement over the phone? A witness testimony carried out over the phone can cover a wide range of evidence saving you from hours of sitting in traffic.

Sometimes, a Learner only rarely carries out a task that forms part of the requirement. If this is the case, a witness testimony may be the only way you can gather evidence to cover the criteria.

This is when preparation pays off, if you have the witness' contact details (gained from your first meeting) and have your Witness Testimony Template in front of you, you will easily conduct a witness testimony which can be digitally recorded.

You then have the required evidence, with an audit trail which can be authenticated.

Authentication of Evidence

Evidence sent to you by the Learner can quickly be authenticated by a witness via a phone call; this saves a great deal of time and traveling to and from your Learners' place of work.

Remember to seek the witness's permission to record the conversation.

Also remember to include the time and date together with the witness's name and contact details within the introduction to the testimony.

Key Points

The telephone is the most under-valued assessment tool.

The telephone can save you hours of travelling.

Record all telephone communication; recording devices are widely available over the internet.

Inform the Learner or witness that you are recording the conversation.

Record the Learner or witness's name and contact details to provide an audit trail.

The Post

Many Learners do not have mobile phones or access to the internet, for them the postal system is the only way to communicate.

A first class letter posted one day will arrive at its destination the very next day. The Learner doesn't even need to be in, the letter just lands on the doormat waiting for the Learner to read it.

Using the post, you can remind the Learner to send you evidence. If you enclose a stamped addressed envelope, the Learner has no excuse.

The Learner can send a variety of evidence through the post, including; photos, documents and the written answers to the knowledge questions.

A learner can also return documentation that has been signed such as Reviews and updated Assessment Plans.

When sending documents through the post it is always best to keep a copy as documents sometimes 'go missing'. It is good practice to phone a few days after posting to ensure your Learner has received their mail. A follow-up phone call also acts as a prompt to return documents etc.

Key Points

If documents require signing consider using the post.

Always supply a stamped addressed envelope for the Learner to return your documents.

Keep a track of all outgoing and incoming post in-case mail goes 'missing'.

Be proactive, phone your Learner to confirm they have received the documents.

Assessment Decisions, Why make them?

As assessors, we have to make decisions as to whether or not a Learner is competent.

Assessment Decisions are an essential part of the Assessment process and an invaluable aide to assessment.

The process of making an assessment decision forces you to focus on the requirements of the qualification and allow you to identify any criteria which require additional evidence.

Now is the time to consider how your Learner can provide this for you. You could, for instance; ask your Learner take photos of products and forward them to you (together with the contact details of a reliable witness. You could then use the photos as a basis of a professional discussion.

Contact the witness to authenticate the Product and professional discussion.

Key Points

Making an assessment decision forces the decision 'is there sufficient evidence?'

How can the Learner get evidence to prove competence?

Learner Feedback, Why Give It?

Learner feedback is an essential tool in the assessor tool-bag. As far as this book is concerned, the primary function of giving the Learner feedback is to encourage the Learner to gather sufficient, usable, evidence to prove their competence.

Encourage the Learner. Keep the Learner involved in their qualification. Show the Learner how easily they can gather evidence for their qualification. Create a 'wish list' of evidence you want and discuss with your Learner how they could get the required evidence.

Arrange for the Learner to have the evidence for you before the next visit or, better still get the Learner to post or email evidence to you or even better get your Learner to upload the evidence onto an e-portfolio for you.

If you need to observe a criteria make sure the Learner realises the importance of contacting you so that you can arrange an assessment visit at a suitable time.

Positive feedback should inspire the Learner and an inspired Learner will gather evidence for you thereby making your life easier and more efficient.

An un-inspired Learner may lose interest, find excuses for not completing the knowledge questions or even fail to tell the assessor when they change jobs, move home or change phone numbers. Due to any one of these factors a Learner may 'drop from the radar' and fail to complete their qualification.

It is therefore essential to enthuse the Learner, keep them on program and complete their qualification, thus ensuring your centre maintains high rates of timely completions.

High success rates and timely completions are crucial to maintain your centre's funding streams.

Key Points

Positive feedback will engage the Learner.

An engaged Learner will gather evidence for you.

Give the Learner sufficient information to enable you both to work out an assessment strategy whereby the Learner can produce the evidence for you.

Reviewing the Learner's Progress & Updating the Assessment Plan

Constantly review the Learners progress, this allows you to focus on the criteria which need more evidence. Keeping the Learner informed of their progress enables both you and the Learner to plan how you can gather the evidence.

Consider the range of assessment methods your Learner can use to gather valid, authentic and safe evidence to demonstrate their competence in the qualification.

With a little encouragement your Learner should be able to produce photos of products and copies of documents etc. A colleague could take photos and shoot videos. Your Learner can ask employers, clients and customers to produce references and witness testimonies etc.

Consider what evidence can be gathered remotely. You can record witness's testimonies over the phone and you can phone employers to ask for references. Clients can be contacted and they too can provide evidence to cover a wide range of criteria.

As a final resort, consider returning to the venue to carry out further assessments. An assessment plan can always be arranged over the phone and adapted to suite changing circumstances. Make sure you allow for any eventuality in your planning.

Key Points

Continually monitor your Learners' progress

Keep your Learner informed and engaged.

Plan for the Learner to gather as much evidence for you as possible.

Allow for any changes of circumstances.

The Assessor Toolbox 1
The Mobile Phone

The mobile phone is an amazing multi-use tool; it's like a 21st Century Swiss Army Knife. The convenience of the mobile phone is matched only by its usefulness. It fits snugly in the pocket and has a range of tools that are perfectly suited to gathering evidence. It can even be used for phoning and texting Learners!

Your Learners can take photos and text them to you, together with witness phone numbers. You can then carry out an assessment from the comfort of your armchair.

Use the digital voice recorder on your mobile phone to record professional discussions, witness testimonies and observations.
An observation recorded onto your phone can save you hours writing reports, just upload the audio file onto your e-portfolio where the evidence can be time stamped and quickly referenced with 'bullet points'.

The mobile phone is almost designed for gathering video evidence. A short video clip can provide evidence covering a wide range of performance criteria and is quick and easy to upload, time-stamp and reference onto your e-portfolio.

Make sure you to store a Learner's contact details and photo on your phone.

Use their contact details to phone before leaving the office for an assessment visit.

Your Learner's photo acts as an aide memoir to help you identify them when you arrive at the assessment venue.

Key Points

Make full use of mobile phones.

Encourage your Learner to take photos, shoot videos and record witness testimonies.

Phone the Learners' supervisor to record a witness testimony.

Phone the Learner to ensure an assessment visit can go ahead.

Use your mobile phone to take photos, shoot videos, record discussions and witness testimonies.

Store your Learners' details (including photo) on your mobile as an aide memoir when visiting the Learner.

The Assessor Toolbox 2
The Electronic Portfolios

E-portfolios have revolutionised the way we work.

We no longer have to write and reference our reports by hand, entering the same information time and time again. Cross-referencing from reports to Unit pages to reviews is all done for you, saving you massive amounts of time. A wide range of evidence including photos, video and audio recordings can simply be dropped into the e-portfolio and laborious tasks such as, producing a list of the criteria that still requires evidence, can be done with the click of the mouse.

E-portfolios increase efficiency and productivity, they save you time and help you avoid mistakes due to errors when cross-referencing. E-portfolios save your college time and money. There is no time wasted printing out and assembling paper-portfolios and space wasted archiving bulky portfolios.

E-portfolios also help to save the planet! They reduce the amount of paper and toner we use thereby helping us reduce our carbon footprint.

Key Points

An e-portfolio will make you more efficient.

Test Drive the Intelligent Portfolio.

The Assessor Toolbox 3 the Intelligent Portfolio

Development of the **IntelligentPortfolio** been driven by the needs and requirements of the users; Learners, assessors, the quality assurance team and the management.

The Learner;
The Learner can simply logon to the Learner Portal from their Smart phone, Android, IPad, Iphone, computer or laptop. They can see their progress on a pie chart, read a message from their tutor, complete tasks and upload files, documents, photos or video etc. for your tutor to mark.

The easy to use Learner Portal

The Assessor;
Work On-Line or work Off-Line
You can use the IntelligentPortfolio off line;
You do not need an internet connection to work on your portfolios. This gives you the freedom to work where there is a limited or poor internet connection.

An additional bonus of being internet free is the almost instant uploading of video evidence.

Easy to Use
The IntelligentPortfolio is easy to quick and easy to use. Video Evidence is easily uploaded. Videos can be viewed and referenced and 'Time Stamped'.

Report writing is aided with a variety of 'Text Tools' including; 'Spell-checker', 'Quotes' (used to insert often used phrases) and 'Text Drag' (used to move text and referencing within the report).

Reviews
Reviews are simplified thanks to an instant overview of the criteria that has been met.
One click enters the required evidence and another, the assessment methods.
Input panels for comments etc speed up the review process.

Completion Documentation
Pre-populated completion documentation saves the assessor entering assessment data saving yet more time.

The simple layout of the Intelligent Portfolio.

Start by selecting a Learner; view their Contact and Registration Details, their photo, and their progress on each Unit.

Add private notes on your Learner such as 'Learner is dyslexic must carry-out knowledge questioning away from colleagues.

For the Quality Assurance Team;

The Intelligent Portfolio has a range of features designed to help you monitor Learners and simplify the quality assurance process.

Overview of Learner Progress

You simply select an assessor and are presented with an instant overview of their Learners' progress.

Colour coding (amber and red) identifies any Learner that has not been reviewed within four and eight weeks.

Colour coding also identifies Learners approaching and passed their expected end date.

The Overview of Learner Progress

Sampling

You can select any portfolio documents to view from a list. Evidence and referencing is easily viewed and checked against criteria.

Time is saved when you sample video or audio evidence thanks to the 'time skip' function; by clicking on a time on the 'Time Line', the video (or audio) skips to the selected time.

Notes and Action Points can be added to a report at any time whilst sampling the portfolio.

Sampling Video Evidence

Sampling Reports

A copy of the sampling report is sent via the internal messaging system to the Assessor to countersign. When countersigned, a copy of the report is stored in the Sampling Report Folder for audit.

For the Manager;

The development of the Manager part of the system has also been driven by the user. You have all the features available to the Quality Assurance Team, plus all the tools required for the easy administration of the assessment and quality assurance process, including bulk loading of Learners by CSV file, Certification and Archiving.

Key Points

Try the  for free*.

Free Learner portfolios for you to trial with your Learners*.

Free Demonstration and Training*.

Phone 020 337 11995

www.hhgsol.com

Assessing Video Evidence

Assessing video evidence is easy using the Intelligent Portfolio.

Simply load the video you want to reference. The video plays immediately.

Pause the video when you want to reference a criteria. Double click in the 'Time Line' to insert the time

Write your description into the report.

To reference the line of text click on the button next to the text line ▢, This takes you to the Unit pages where you can click on the criteria you wish to reference.

Reviewing Learner Progress

Reviewing Learner progress and updating Assessment Plan is quick, easy and accurate using the Intelligent Portfolio.

A panel displays the percentage completed of each Unit. The 'Override' button takes the percentage up to 100%.

Another panel shows the Evidence covered since the last review.

Click on the Unit button to insert the Units and Criteria to be assessed on the next visit

Next select the Assessment Methods to add them to the Review.

Finally add your comments for the Learner

A Brief History of the Intelligent Portfolio

INTELLIGENTPORTFOLIO™

We began as a small assessment centre assessing construction workers for their NVQ's.

Knowing that e-portfolios would make our lives easier and more efficient we tried several leading e-portfolios, however none of them did as we wanted. They were all difficult to use and needed an internet connection.

To keep things simple, we decided to convert our paper-based portfolio to an electronic version.

We began by installing the portfolio onto our computers, thus avoiding the necessity of having to connect to the internet. An advantage of this was that we didn't get 'timed out' when trying to upload large video files. Another advantage was, we were not affected when one of the 'cloud' based e-portfolio systems crashed (this happened on a regular basis during the busy periods at the end of the academic year).

We developed a range of features to help us write and reference our reports, making sure we maintained a simple and easy to use desktop.

We quickly realised that we could use the data we created during referencing to speed up the review process.

We needed a simple and easy to use portal for our Learners to remotely complete their knowledge questions. They also needed to be able to upload evidence such as photos or videos that they had produced.

We had the web-based Learner Portal built enabling Learners to log on with their smart phones, Ipads and tablets (as well as with p.c.'s and laptops).

For the Quality Assurance Team we developed the IQA part of the program, building in a range of features including one that allows us to view evidence (such as photos, documents and videos) while we made our reports.

We also developed our unique 'Time Stamp' feature which allows the IQA to skip to specific Time Stamped sections of video and audio evidence when sampling portfolios. This saves a great deal of time, especially when some of our Professional Discussions are 45 minutes long!

As centre manager I wanted to make my life easier.
We developed a desktop that allows centre managers to monitor Learner activity and progress in real time. This allows me to identify any issues before they become problems

Various features and functions simplify the management processes, giving me more time to manage the assessors and quality assurance teams.

During the development phase, the Intelligent Portfolio was continually tested by the users.

Any ideas for improvements were discussed and implemented. Problems were identified and resolved.

We also took the Intelligent Portfolio to other providers to evaluate. Their feedback was invaluable and led to us giving the Intelligent Portfolio a cosmetic overhaul and further simplification.

The Intelligent Portfolio is now being used in several colleges and private providers.

Going Forward

The goal of this book was to demonstrate a different approach to assessment. To encourage the use of Dynamic Assessment methods, to embrace new technology and use remote assessment methods to reduce the time wasted travelling to and from assessment venues and minimize the environmental impact of such unnecessary travel. Hopefully you are now enthusiastically planning how you can put the ideas expressed in this book into action.

Good luck and happy assessing,

Andy Wells.

Remember the 6 golden rules;

1   Know your Standards inside out, see how the Units cross-over and inter-relate.

2   Always assess holistically across the Units.

3   Use Dynamic Assessing to identify evidence and assessment opportunities.

4   Carry out 'Virtual' Assessment Visits' whenever possible.

5   Embrace technology and see how you can use it to your advantage.

6   Try the Intelligent Portfolio.

Made in the USA
Charleston, SC
31 May 2014